WRITING & REVISING
YOUR FICTION

Writing & Revising Your Fiction

✍ ✍ ✍

by Mark Wisniewski

✍ ✍ ✍

Boston   THE WRITER, INC.   *Publishers*

Library of Congress Cataloging-in-Publication Data

Wisniewski, Mark S.
    Writing and revising your fiction / by
Mark Wisniewski.
        p.   cm.
    ISBN 0-87116-174-5 : $12.00
    1. Fiction—Technique. I. Title.
    PN3355.W57   1995
808.3—dc20   94-37234
                                              CIP

Printed in the United States of America

CONTENTS

Preface

Before You Begin

IF YOU'RE THE TYPICAL underpublished writer, no one ever asked you to write. Still, you feel the call to put short stories or novels on paper. Unfortunately—for the potential readers of the fine fiction within you—sometimes that call seems to fade.

The purpose of this book is to provide the boost you need to keep you writing your way toward success; to answer *how* questions; to help you maintain discipline. It will probably work best for you if you know the assumptions on which the book is based.

The first is that writing fiction is a multi-step process. That might not be news to you, but it's a good notion to keep in mind now and then, especially if you tend to skip steps—or rush through revision.

Second, the individual writing process that works optimally for you is not precisely the same as anyone else's. Each writer's combination of writing strengths and weaknesses is different, so the specific chain of "tricks" you use to enhance your strengths and minimize your weaknesses will be unique. Moreover, the process by which you will produce your best fiction can change from project to project: If writing a rough draft is your biggest problem today, it may be your greatest strength six months from now.

The third assumption is that repeated revision is what distinguishes fiction enough to make it publishable. Two chapters (eight and nine) offer revision tips; both also suggest that revising in itself provides "lifelong learning" on a subject that's difficult to master fully.

Finally, there's the assumption that success in fiction writing is difficult for beginners to achieve, but that anyone can raise his or her fiction to publishable quality. As long as you are willing to make the necessary effort, you are certain to improve your stories and novels.

As you read this book, you'll notice that *listing* can help you at several stages of writing; it is a time-efficient, low-pressure activity. (Simply jotting words down in columns *feels* easier than struggling to create wonderful sentences.)

You'll also notice an insistence on *writing activity.* Talking about writing—an activity many wanna-be writers enjoy— merely saps the time writers should be using to write. If you spend spare time putting words on paper, you'll succeed far sooner than the people who talk about writers' angst in coffee shops.

You need to remain flexible as you write your fiction. Follow the prescribed exercises, and adopt those that work well for you, but always be prepared for your fiction to write itself. This phenomenon won't occur during all of your writing projects—in fact, it may never happen—but when it does, loosen the reins and enjoy the ride.

Think of this book as an exercise partner: Sometimes it'll push you harder than you want, but that might be just what you need. And if you feel so inclined, take notes in the margins of this book. After all, it's never too early to begin writing.

—Mark Wisniewski

WRITING & REVISING
YOUR FICTION

*"The best fiction illuminates
similarities between people who are
commonly thought of as different."*

‖ 1

Creating Vital
Characters

S UBMITTING FICTION for publication is a series of
offers and acceptances—or denials—regarding emotion, diction, values, and, yes, even sometimes politics. You, the fiction writer, capture these
elements in your work and send it to an editor. On
a good day, you connect: You find an editor who
appreciates your characters and believes they will
give readers emotional or intellectual stimulation—
and you receive an acceptance letter. On a bad day,

your main character reminds an editor of his or her worst enemy, and you receive a rejection slip. On a so-so day, an editor admires your work but returns it, probably without telling you why, possibly without realizing why, often because the characters didn't seem to be *breathing*.

These so-so days should concern you as you create characters for your next fiction piece. Your good days, obviously, have taken care of themselves. And as for the bad days, you cannot control an editor's dislikes, family experiences, political views, hatreds, and loves. In fact, if your characters have drawn a strong reaction, you've probably characterized well. Perhaps what you need is better targeting—finding an editor who appreciates the way your characters think.

How do you avoid the so-so days? Three suggestions might help. First, study what made your good days good. Second, don't let your bad days get the best of you. Finally, don't underestimate important advice you've previously ignored: Do not write your next piece without creating character dossiers.

To begin, reread the passages about the characters in your successful fiction as if you were a satisfied editor. What made your characters sparkle? How did you describe them specifically and portray their desires? Did you use spontaneous yet precise dialogue? What thoughts did your characters have that were fresh, appealing, and engaging?

To answer these questions completely, reread not only the final draft of your successful story; study your rough and middle drafts as well, then try to repeat your success. Remember that you are developing *your* voice and vision, not Hemingway's or Woolf's—and that failure awaits writers who try to replicate the voices of legendary authors. The editor appreciated *you* at your best, so figure out what you did well and work to repeat that performance—with a new twist—in your next story. This advice might seem obvious, but for some reason, writers rarely practice it. So get ahead of the game by doing again what has worked before.

The second way to fight so-so days is by getting rid of your fear of portraying "unlikable" characters. To begin this process, consider the following proposition: Editors who label characters as "unlikable" are only saying, "I didn't like those people." This simply means that if you send these characters elsewhere, a different editor might find them engaging. Once you become shy and defensive about your characters—once you begin making them evasive or unwilling to behave in a distinctive way or speak boldly about what's on their minds—they will lose their vitality and uniqueness.

Vitality should be your goal when you create characters. Vitality is more difficult to create than popularity. It takes more thought, revision, trial-and-error, drafts, insight into the human condition, work, speculation, hope, and willingness to ignore the conventions and traditions that prescribe that "good" people speak and think in a particular manner. Vital characters, however, capture your readers' interest and attention, and help produce a dramatic plot. They humor and stimulate readers and impress editors who might otherwise admire your writing but nevertheless reject your work.

A third way to prevent so-so days depends on your giving character development priority in your writing. Aristotle believed that plot was paramount—that it should be conceived before other story elements—but many contemporary fiction writers would disagree, arguing that the most important element of a story is character. You can mesh Aristotle's wisdom with contemporary literary opinion by proceeding in your fiction writing on the presumption that in a good story, plot and character are intertwined.

To give characters priority in your writing, create your main characters first; then let them struggle to make their way into the action. Forget about writing a first sentence; instead, make a character dossier.

A dossier is a list of attributes that a particular character *might* have. It involves physical descriptions as well as likes, dislikes, habits, family history, recurring dreams, failed dates, unwise friendships and relationships, worries, bad memories, hopes, favorite foods, speeding tickets, and, most crucially, *desires.* It should not read as factually as a personals ad or a resumé; it should include inconsistencies and offer surprises and quirks—as do most interesting people.

Character dossiers take time to develop, but they save time in the long run because they help you create characters who have stories behind them, which means less extensive revision and fewer rejections. If writing dossiers puts you off, try having fun with them. Remember, you don't have to include everything from them in the fiction you ultimately write. And if having to write a dossier for each of your characters makes you want to cut down the number of characters in your story or novel, do so. If you don't care enough about a character to write a dossier about him or her, that character probably doesn't belong in your story.

To begin to create a dossier, write a possible name for the character at the top of a blank sheet of paper (or computer screen), then list as quickly as possible words or phrases that *might* describe that character. Don't worry about spelling or elegance; and don't erase, cross out, or delete. Personalities, remember, are sloppy. Surrender to the momentum of listing, and save your concerns about form for later. If you write ten entries and don't like them, don't worry. Keep listing, and you will eventually be satisfied. If you get stuck, glance at the name at the top of the page or scan the items on the list to this point; they'll spark related phrases or words. If you're still stuck, think of yourself as a creator putting together a spiral of DNA. Enjoy the freedom of random selection and the power of building complication.

As an example, here's a section of a 100-entry list conceived in less than ten minutes:

Herman Contrarian
    1) hates his name
    2) wears five silver rings on left hand

  *3) loves salsa
   4) only child
   5) tolerates war
   6) black hair dyed red
   7) uses shampoos marked FOR DRY, LIFELESS HAIR
   8) 28 years old
   9) hates to put on socks
  *10) wants to invent something useful and expensive
   11) met main character a year before story began
   12) born in Anchorage, Alaska
   13) has never had a physical
   14) coughs a lot
  *15) mail-orders $50 worth of vitamins a month
   16) can't stand sweet pickles
   17) is a vegetarian
   18) reddish mole on left earlobe
   19) sleeps until 11:00 AM
   20) works as bartender on M Street
   21) detests sports except for hockey
   22) mother had three miscarriages before he was born
  *23) still loves Anna Belle, whom he knew in high school
   24) has had four dates in life

The asterisks highlight this character's *desires,* which will create sympathy and spark plot-complicating action. Use asterisks to make sure your character has at least five significant desires.

If this procedure for developing characters leaves you blocked as you begin your next piece of fiction, try these practical tips:

1) Don't write about yourself. You know yourself too well—or sometimes not well enough—to portray yourself artfully. As an author, you should love your characters though they are unlike you—and know them even better than you know yourself.

2) If you feel you are so fascinating that you belong in your fiction, make yourself a minor character. Then fictionalize at least half the details on that character's dossier.

3) Study famous people. Notice that many are both strongly liked *and* disliked. Ask yourself what this tells you about character "likability."

4) Accept the fact that a dossier is necessary for you to write publishable fiction. Don't make the mistake of most writers who are "stuck" in their careers: Don't tell yourself that dossiers are for beginners only.

5) Rather than making a 100-entry dossier, try one with 1,000 entries, and revise it by crossing out and rewording entries—even changing the character's name at the top. Take advantage of the fact that dossiers list *potential* characteristics, and that characters, like people, are alive and therefore subject to change.

6) If a plot, or a scene, or even an interesting fictional event occurs to you while you're writing a

dossier, work it into your list somehow, then consider taking time out to jot it down in your journal. Though doing so may distract you from the momentum of listing, when you go back to your dossier, your momentum will be stronger, fueled by new ideas of what will *happen*. If events begin dominating your list but you don't want to quit listing, so be it: Any writing that does more than one thing at the same time is probably good writing.

7) Don't ever throw away a character's dossier or tell yourself a dossier is finished. Adding to your list while you are writing a rough draft—or a second draft, or a third—can only help your fiction. Some writers add to dossiers even after the work in which those characters appear has been published. That's what's called love of character. And sometimes that's how novels and trilogies and movie sequels develop.

8) Once you've conceived a character, portray him or her from the point of view of someone who is extremely different from you—perhaps that of your worst enemy. Always keep in mind that the best fiction illuminates similarities between people who are commonly thought of as different.

9) Do a revision, making a minor character major.

10) Write an imaginary conversation between you and your characters.

11) Give your main character a political agenda, and let him or her speak about it for a page of free writing. Consider revising the result and submitting it as a letter to the editor. Then, in

order to let your characters show their quirkiest qualities, force them to promise never to let that agenda surface in your work.

12) Indicate on your dossier which details about your character arise from his or her *inner voice* (thoughts) and which arise from his or her *outer voice* (dialogue). Note the differences between these voices, and highlight those differences as you write and revise your text.

13) Above all, take advantage of the fact that by studying successful characters, by forgetting "bad days," and by creating dossiers, serious fiction writers are creating a love for characters who will enthuse them to write and review. This enthusiasm results not only in sharply drawn characters, but also in final drafts of stories and novels with compelling sentences, dialogue, drama, suspense, and plot. Love of character is contagious: If the writer has it, it will affect his or her work, and eventually, at least one editor.

"All plots can be reduced to either of two situations: Stranger Comes to Town, or Hero Embarks on a Journey."

‖ 2

Plotting: Events Within Events

HAVE YOU EVER BEEN interrupted while telling an anecdote to a group of friends? If so, you probably knew that, after the interruption, your friends would either say, "And then what happened?"—or turn the conversation onto a different path. If they said, "Then what?" you could have justifiably felt the pride of an accomplished storyteller. If they began a new topic, you just did not make your audience want to hear more.

To produce satisfying fiction, writers must give readers reason to want to *read* more. They must know that readers are interrupted by phone calls and everyday demands; that reading is an investment of their time and concentration; and if the story doesn't capture their attention at the outset, they stop reading.

When plots involve conflict, suspense, and an exciting climax, readers want to read on. Well-written fiction with appealing characters may fail to get into print because it lacks one or more of these elements. Writers often know this but don't know what to do about it. Some try "inserting" these elements into drafts, only to find that the story will seem forced, and the process frustrating for them.

To create plots that keep readers reading, writers should make "event chains" *before* they write a rough draft. Event chains are lists of events that may or may not happen in a piece of fiction. They are to plot what character dossiers are to character.

To make an event chain, study your character dossiers to see what your characters want. If these dossiers don't list the characters' goals or desires, expand them until they do. Then begin your event chain by making a list of at least fifteen events that *could* happen, making sure your characters' desires are part of this list. For example, create a situation in which Character A wants something Character B has, or Character A needs Character B to get something Character C wants, or A wants B to change, or A simply wants B.

List these events in chronological order, regardless of how or whether they'll appear in your finished manuscript. If irrelevant events pop up on your list, don't worry: Future events on the list might make them relevant. And: You can always *omit* events when you come to the actual writing. What's important is that you have enough events to make sure that conflict will exist in your fiction.

To make sure that your fiction will have a satisfying climax, see that your event chain includes several "magic moments," points at which the reader anticipates an event that can lead to a number of possible results, each with some degree of positive or negative outcome for the characters.

An example of a magic moment might be a last-second shot by a basketball player whose team is down by a point. Like readers hooked on a story, people watching the game at that moment are attentive and entertained because they don't know whether the ball will go through the hoop, but they *do* know that the shot will determine the game's outcome. They also know that, after the shot, players will respond emotionally. Coaches might be fired; the crowd will scream, go silent, or rush out onto the floor.

In fiction, magic moments rise from mental decision-making as well as physical action. They are most satisfying when they rise from characters' desires, though sometimes they come from the setting. The more magic moments in your story, the better—because each of them, by engaging the reader emotionally, counteracts the threat of interruption.

On your event chain, put stars next to your magic moments. Put two stars next to those that may become your climax, the magic moment at which the clash among your characters' goals is most complex and threatening. If you don't have such a point, add more events until you do; or if this doesn't work, make a new, more specific list— perhaps one including goals you had previously considered "minor." When this requires you to lengthen your character dossiers, or create a new character with yet another dossier, do so. You're better off spending time making additional entries than writing a story or novel with an uninteresting plot.

Here's the event chain I made before writing a short story called "Birthday":

1) In the middle of the night, Jeff begins walking down the stairs from his bedroom and hears his parents arguing about their checking account.

2) Jeff wants the argument to stop.

*3) He hears his father, an unemployed construction worker, say they shouldn't have adopted Kim, Jeff's five-year-old sister.

4) The following morning, which is Kim's birthday, Jeff finds cancelled checks on the kitchen floor, apparently the result of his parents' argument. He traces a signature from a check to forge a note that says he must be excused from school early so he can take Kim to see a doctor.

*5) Jeff shows the note to his teacher.

6) She agrees to an early dismissal.

*7) Jeff shows the note to Kim's teacher.

8) She agrees. Jeff takes Kim for a ride on his bike and tells her they are going some place to make money.

9) Kim asks Jeff if he can buy her "the little doll" she wants.

10) Jeff says they are going to get enough money to buy a "big doll." He bikes to a lake where his father and he took down a wealthy man's pier the previous fall.

11) Jeff has Kim crawl through the tiny unlocked window of the tool shed on the property and open the door for Jeff, so he can enter and "borrow" a fishing rod the wealthy man keeps there.

12) Jeff digs up worms and begins catching bluegills. It is May—just after spawning—so the fish bite furiously. Kim loves playing with the fish and is intrigued by their colors.

*13) An old neighbor comes out and scolds Jeff for fishing out the spawning nests.

*14) Jeff tells the man that it's Kim's birthday, and asks if he can fish on the man's property.

*15) The man agrees, then leaves.

16) The man returns with a large bucket for Kim to use to keep the fish alive.

17) When the bucket is full of fish, Jeff returns the pole to the shed, hangs the bucket on the bike's handle bars, puts Kim behind him on the bike, and

rides to a building where, according to grade school rumor, "people buy and sell fish."

**18) Kim loses her balance on the bike seat, and as Jeff turns to help her, they both fall onto the highway.

19) Jeff and Kim gather up the fish, which, without water, begin to die.

*20) The place to which they are going to sell the fish is run by a seafood wholesaler. By then the fish are dead, and a man on the loading dock says they aren't worth much.

*21) Jeff says he wants to sell them anyway.

22) The man offers him eleven cents a pound.

23) Jeff tells the man that's not as much as he wanted.

**24) The man tells Jeff to take the fish away.

25) Jeff accepts the man's offer, but is not paid enough to buy the small doll Kim wants.

26) Jeff drives Kim home on his bike.

This list has more plot events than necessary for one story. Some are action-oriented; some involve the suspense of the characters' hearts and minds. Because I wasn't committed to any one event, I felt free to focus only on those relevant to the story I wanted to write. What was important was that I played with possibilities *quickly*—and enjoyed doing so.

Note that there are several magic moments in this list, and when characters ask one another for favors related to their desires, magic moments ensue—because, depending on the answer, events can proceed on various different tangents. I identified potential climaxes and put two stars beside numbers eighteen and twenty-four. In these events, the tangling of several wants could spark a number of significant possibilities for *several* characters.

Once you've listed enough events to produce your climax, look at *sections* of the list and decide which would make your best plot. Good fiction usually climaxes near its end, so if your sixth event is your climax, events two through eight might be all you need for the best narrated work of fiction. Study your list critically to determine which section you should actually develop into a story. Would your third event bore your readers? Wouldn't they probably *assume* event two? What if you narrated only events four through seven? Would the first event work best as a flashback or slipped into dialogue? What if you turned your potential climax into a whole story or novel by dividing it into several "sub-events" (events within the event)? What if the climax happened *before* your story actually began? Could the aftermath make better fiction than the explosion itself?

After you've found your most promising group of events, make a list that divides these events into sub-events. Include thoughts, lines of dialogue, or gestures; again, include more possibilities than you'll probably use. If your list veers toward strange events, let it: After all, it's only a list. Look at sections of this new list as possibilities for several fiction pieces; create as many sub-events in these sections as you can.

Theoretically, you can divide lists and create new lists of sub-events until your entries begin to suggest paragraphs, sentences, or even phrases. But you don't have to continue to refine your events to that extent. You need only make your lists increasingly specific until a chain of events emerges that seems to demand that you begin writing.

When you write your rough draft, do so briskly. Don't worry about grammar, spelling, punctuation, or poetic prose; you can edit for those later. Let your enthusiasm about what will happen spill onto your paper or screen. If you want to skip ahead because you're excited about a given event on your list, do so. If your manuscript begins to move away from your event chain, let that happen as long as you feel enthused. Nine out of ten times, enthusiasm in drafting translates into tension, suspense, and heightened reader interest. It also often produces fresh, tight, interesting sentences that need less revision than sentences "perfected" during breaks from rough draft writing.

Creating event chains saves time. Deleting one entry from a list is faster than writing and deleting a page of your manuscript. Event chains also prevent writer's block, because if you've made enough of them before you began drafting, you have nuggets on which to build. This early work also prevents "rough draft slump," that feeling of aimlessness that often hits in the middle of drafting—because if you've cut out unnecessary events before you begin writing, your narrative is less likely to sag.

If you've followed the above advice and your plot still needs improvement, here are some practical tips to consider:

1) A story or novel works out best if it begins in the middle of action, and if you establish what your main character wants—but cannot have—in the first few sentences.

2) Consider the theory that all plots can be reduced to either of two situations: Stranger Comes to Town, or Hero Embarks on a Journey. Try reshaping your plot to fit it into one of these formulas, and explore the various plot twists that result. Notice that at the core of both formulas is the potential for narrative *momentum*.

3) In the best fiction, two or more events happen simultaneously. After you've devised one plot line, think of another and figure out how to present both at the same time.

4) Let your fiction raise questions in readers' minds, but answer these questions as you go along. Each answer should come up early so readers won't be annoyed—but late enough to make them keep reading.

5) If you begin a story or novel but can't work out a satisfactory ending, try to envision an interesting scene or event and figure out how to bring your readers into that scene. In other words, create your plot backwards.

6) If you're in the middle of writing a piece of fiction, but can't figure out how to get to the next scene, go back and add details as you revise.

7) Suspense is evoked most easily by action

and/or dialogue. If you aren't using specific words and gestures to tell your story, dissect your *sentences* and present them in the tiniest "bites" possible.

8) Remember that plot events can occur in characters' minds—especially as characters reach decisions. Don't be afraid to narrate the drama of thought.

9) As you render magic moments, don't reverse the chronological order of naturally suspenseful events. For example, don't write, "Before I saw my winning lottery numbers on the TV screen, I was sweating." Write, "I was sweating. The first lottery number popped onto the screen."

10) Cut out "hint" words. In the sentence, "Jack's car slid hopelessly across the icy lot, but then stopped short of damaging the Mercedes," the words "hopelessly" and "but" reduce the possible outcomes drastically, and therefore kill suspense before the reader is presented with the outcome. This scene would be much more suspenseful if it read, "Jack's car slid across the ice toward the Mercedes. The man in the Mercedes frowned; Jack felt impact; the man got out of the Mercedes, inspected the bumpers, and yelled, 'You were lucky.'"

11) Give your characters deadlines by which time they must achieve their goal. Put a clock on the wall in one—or all—of your scenes.

12) Don't "tease" your reader. Allow your suspense to run high, but when it crests, let one beat of time pass, and then quickly deliver the surprise.

13) Keep in mind that plot is a matter of allowing characters to pursue what they are after,

then visualize your story as a high-hurdle race. Set a goal with plenty of hurdles that may or may not trip the runners. Picture them running quickly enough to hold the attention of a reader with the shortest attention span. As a writer, you must make sure that the runners *want* to run, that there are no false starts, that the hurdles are the optimal height, and that, toward the end of your story, several runners are straining to reach the finish line and break the ribbon.

"Don't worry about telling your story through the senses and mind of someone whose personality is not at all like yours; be grateful for the chance to explore."

‖ 3

Point of View: Your Options

POINT OF VIEW may be your most important consideration as you conceive your story; it can make the difference between dull and riveting fiction, even if you have fascinating characters and an engaging plot. It is essential for you to understand the concept of point of view and to take time to choose the best one for your fiction.

Consider the various personalities involved when you write fiction: 1) you, the writer; 2) your narrator; and 3) the other characters in your story or novel. As you write, make clear who's who. You, the writer, are *not* the narrator. Your narrator is a character, but is distinct from other characters.

This established, study your dossiers and event lists for the person who can narrate your fiction most convincingly. Could a minor character, somewhat distanced from your major character's thoughts and goals, tell your story or novel best? Could the fact that someone does *not* know all of the events on your event chain inject tension into the story he or she could tell? Does your main character know a fact about your narrator that this narrator hasn't learned? Would your readers enjoy knowing—or want to know—that secret? Could the age, humor, or emotional state of a certain character add "edge" to a narrative told through that character's eyes?

Search for your ideal point of view until one sparks enthusiasm in you. Don't worry about telling your story through the senses and mind of someone whose personality is not at all like yours; be grateful for the chance to *explore.*

Once you've chosen your point of view character—let's say his name is George—consider *how* he will narrate the events in the story. One option is *third-person* narration, sometimes called the "reporting" narration, where "he" or "she" is the predominant pronoun. Example: "George sat staring at the hole in his ceiling; he scratched his scalp; he was waiting for Aunt Bernice." The advantage of third-person point of view is that it allows you significant leeway in what you write. Your sentences can focus closely on George's thoughts or "pull back"—like a movie camera—to describe a scene panoramically. Its disadvantage is that, if you don't use this leeway skillfully, your readers might feel emotionally distant from your characters.

Third-person narration can be either *omniscient* or *limited.* If *omniscient,* George's narration could—magically—relate your story through the mind and eyes of any of your characters; his narrative could skip from scene to scene and quote anyone's dialogue and present any character's thoughts.

Even when written and revised well, omniscient third-person narration is inadvisable because, realistically speaking, George *cannot* know everything. Moreover, knowing everything is boring. Good fiction is like interesting gossip: When Aunt Bernice sits at the table to discuss whether Bob Krenshaw is dating too soon after Alice Krenshaw died, George's (and your readers') interest in her lies in hearing the changes in the tone of her voice, watching her facial expressions, wondering why she pauses, noticing that she refuses to make eye contact, imagining what Bob Krenshaw is doing with Winny Maples at that very moment, guessing what Aunt Bernice might say next, and trying, with Aunt Bernice, to piece together the "facts." If George's third-person narrative could magically switch scenes and report that Bob Krenshaw was saying, "Yes, I'm dating Winifield Maples, and I admit I'm doing it too soon after my wife's death," the fun in

Aunt Bernice's gossip would be ruined; your readers would want a new scoop.

Mystery, not knowledge, is what makes gossip good—and fiction shine. For this reason, writers who write in the third person almost always use *limited* narration. This recounts a given scene through *one* specific "he" or "she"; it is "limited" to thoughts and perceptions of that person only.

If you used third-person *limited* viewpoint and George was your point-of-view character, your manuscript might read as follows:

George walks into the kitchen, and Bernice, sitting at the table, quits talking. This is odd, George thinks. I've never known Bernice to sit quietly. "Good evening," he says.

Bernice nods. Her flushed forehead is slick with perspiration; her fingers are picking at the lace tablecloth.

"Did he just walk in?" someone behind the refrigerator asks Bernice. "Did I hear someone else say something?

"It's George," Bernice says. "For a second I thought he might have come here with Bob."

Now I understand, George thinks. "I'm alone," he says. "Go ahead and finish what you were saying."

Everything in this narrative is conveyed through George's senses and mindset. Readers see and hear only what George perceives and thinks; the wording reflects his level of intelligence and way of thinking. These limitations enhance the readers' emotional experience because the readers identify with George.

You can also narrate fiction from the *second person* point of view, in which the predominant pronoun is "you." It is not often used by fiction writers; in fact, Jay McInerney's novel *Bright Lights, Big City* was considered to be somewhat experimental because it was narrated in the second person entirely.

Here's an example of fiction if written from George's point of view, narrated in the second person:

> You walk in the kitchen, and Aunt Bernice stops talking. Odd, you think. I've never known Bernice to sit quietly. "Good evening," you say.
>
> Bernice nods. Her forehead is flushed and slick from perspiration; her fingers fidget with the lace tablecloth.
>
> "Did someone just walk in?" you hear. "Was that just Bob Krenshaw I heard?"
>
> "It's just George," Bernice says, glancing past your face. "Relax."
>
> "Yeah," you say. "Don't mind me. Keep doing whatever you were doing."

Although using second-person viewpoint might catch the attention of editors and readers because it is uncommon, it has the disadvantage of seeming unnatural. The "you"s can become annoying, and your manuscript can sound more like an article than fiction.

The third point of view through which you can narrate your story or novel is the *first person*. Identified by the predominance of the pronoun "I," it is the point of view most commonly used to write memoirs and diaries—and many private-eye mystery novels. Here's an example of first-person narration, from George's point of view:

> Hearing Aunt Bernice's voice, I walked into her kitchen, smelling simmering stuffed cabbage. As soon as she saw me, she stopped talking and folded her hands. That's strange, I thought. I've never known this woman to sit quietly. "Good evening," I said, and she nodded. Her forehead, flushed, was slick from perspiration. Her shiny fingers fidgeted with the lace tablecloth.
>
> "Did someone just walk in?" someone—a woman—said from behind the refrigerator.
>
> "Yeah, but it's not Bob," Bernice said. "You can quit hiding."
>
> "Yeah, relax," I said. "I'm just here to visit and catch up on news."

Many beginning writers find the first-person point of view advantageous because it seems most natural, and they are used to speaking in this style. Furthermore, fiction written in the first person often makes the reader feel close to the narrator— though this sometimes lessens the feeling of closeness to other characters.

Here are some specific reminders about selecting the right point of view:

1) Notice that the differences in the way the events and details were presented in the above examples depended on whether the scene was written

in the first, second, or third person. Take advantage of this: Choose the type of narration that makes it easy for you to write the kind of fiction you are aiming to produce.

2) Be familiar enough with your point of view character to have your narration flow easily, but not to the point that he or she can't surprise you as you write.

3) Once you choose a point of view character, study his or her dossier for hints about how he or she will affect your narration and the other characters. Values, goals, education, birthplace, and residence of a point of view character should affect the narrator's observations, tone, and breadth.

4) Consider reordering the entries on your most recent event chain in light of the point of view character you choose. If he or she causes you to *cut* events from the list, don't worry; just make sure your new event chain includes several magic moments and a strong climax.

5) Next time you find yourself in a crowd, imagine how you might describe the events going on around you through the points of view of the various people you see. Try to put their thoughts and sensory impressions into sentences. Try first-, second-, and third-person narration. *Play* with point of view possibilities to learn how to distinguish them. They need not be confusing. If you let them, they can be fun.

"Voice needn't be formal or 'educated.' If you let it say what it wants to say, it can add rhythm, entertainment, and pace to your fiction."

‖ 4

Selecting Voice

VOICE IS THE sound people imagine when they read a piece of writing. It can be male or female, commanding, timid, wisecracking, childish, wry, shy, or loud; it can connote just about anything. It can sound like someone the reader knows or has heard on a radio. It can make a piece of writing sound alive and vibrant—or hollow and flat.

Recall the last important letter you received from an attorney or the IRS. Did you "hear" someone formal, authoritative, and perhaps commanding, as you read the first few sentences? If not, you should try to develop an "ear" for voice.

Read letters, short stories, novels, phone messages, notes from relatives, shopping lists, classified ads—and write down, for each, at least five "emotion adjectives" that describe the voice. For example, consider the following excerpt from a personal letter, and jot down five adjectives that describe the emotion behind it:

> My stay here hasn't been easy. A day after I arrived, Mike, my host, learned that his mother was going in for emergency bypass surgery. He flew to Arizona to be with her, and I've been staying here by myself ever since.

"Concerned," "informal," "honest," "tense," and "straightforward" convey some of the emotion behind this letter. The words you jotted down were probably different—because each person's mind and imagination are unique.

Do this exercise whenever possible. If, for some pieces of your fiction, your adjectives seem contradictory, that's all to the good; you are "hearing" that the person behind the words is emotionally complex. (For example, "Honey, could you please call Bill right away?" simultaneously conveys sweetness, urgency, and expectation.)

Fiction writers take advantage of the fact that readers hear voice; they strive for a voice distinct enough to call *style*. They develop style by writing, reading, and listening to what they've written, revising, reading and listening again, then writing and rewriting again and again. Once they have developed a distinctive style, it influences their manuscripts. Their word choice, sentence length, and rhythm combine naturally to give their narratives a unique signature.

Advanced fiction writers know, however, when to try to "adopt" a different voice. For example, the dialogue of an uneducated character—to be authentic and distinct from the dialogue of other characters—will probably need to be written in a voice different from a writer's normal narrative style. The words in an interior monologue (thoughts) of a character usually work better if they sound different from a third-person narrative that describes a scene.

A first-person narrative told by a character whose narrative voice would sound different from the writer's style might require the writer to *replicate* a voice consistently throughout a manuscript. Should you face this situation, consider it an opportunity: Adopting someone else's voice for a first-person narrative can make writing easier. Begin this process by listening to the voices of friends, relatives, and radio and television broadcasters. Eavesdrop on strangers' conversations when you're waiting in line at the post office. Take a walk and see if the rhythm of your steps conjures up the cadence of the voice of an old friend. Close your eyes in a quiet room to try to recall songs your aunt sang to you when you were ten. Invent your own method of imagining human speech. If you *enjoy* imagining a certain voice that seems right for the fiction you are writing, your readers probably will also—because your enthusiasm for the "right" voice will most likely result in better writing.

When you've discovered a distinct voice for your point of view character's first-person narrative, you might feel eager to begin your rough draft. That's good. But hold your enthusiasm for an important final step: Try your voice out in a few paragraphs.

Say your point of view character is Sally, a grandmother, and her first-person narrative is about her fifty-year-old son, Lou, a recent convert to Catholicism who goes to his first confession. Your dossier for Lou mentions that he is the black sheep of her family. Before you try to replicate Sally's voice for an entire rough draft, choose an event from your most recent event chain, and write about it in five different styles. Don't worry much about grammar, punctuation, or spelling. Your first try might look—and sound—like this:

So Lou's afraid to go into the confessional. He's fifty years old and he's fought in a war and he can't get himself to go in there. I nod at him but he just keeps kneeling, folding his hands, pretending he's praying. I feel rather confused and perturbed, because I don't wish to interrupt if he's developing his list of sins. However, we've been in the church for an hour, and Father Ruggerio has been waiting in the confessional for half that time, and, at home, a roasting turkey sits in my oven.

Listen to yourself as you read this paragraph out loud. Do the words reflect the voice you wanted to produce? If not, maybe the writing came out sounding a little too formal—Sally wouldn't say "rather confused and perturbed"!—or it may sound too much like the voice you use to write business letters. Don't worry: On the first try, words often don't match the sound in writers' heads. Simply mark up the manuscript, indicating where it rings true and where it doesn't. Take a short break and return to your keyboard and let Sally tell the same event again.

> Here we are, in the beautiful, ornate basilica. I'm praying that Lou makes a good confession because he's got that heart condition, you know—and I want his soul to be pure if anything happens to him when he goes hunting the next day, for gosh sakes—and I open my eyes and see that Lou, my son, is sweating. He's sweating and white-faced, and I whisper, "Louie, go ahead."
>
> "I can't," he says.
>
> "No, go ahead," I tell him. "At some point you have to have faith."

Again: Read it out loud, listen to yourself, and mark up what you've written. Make notes about what you want to change in your next round. Maybe you should let Sally tell the story in the past tense; or, now that Lou himself has spoken, perhaps he's going to have a few more lines of dialogue: After all, the voice you've been imagining does tend to repeat conversations.

Take another break, then return to your paper or screen and try again.

> "Ma," Lou said to me. "I can't for the life of me get myself to stand up."
>
> "What?" I asked him. "Your trick knee again?"
>
> "Don't be silly," he said. "I just don't want to walk into that box."
>
> "Why not, Louie?" I asked. "You fought in a war for gosh sakes."
>
> "And men died in that war," he said. "And they buried them in boxes that looked like that one."
>
> Then I realized that Lou and I weren't whispering: Father Ruggerio could probably hear us through the confessional walls.

When you read this sample aloud, you may feel that the use of past tense makes Sally sound too distant, or that the line about the trick knee *is* silly—to you. Again, mark the sample, noting anything that comes to mind, then take a short break. Then let whatever happens happen:

> I'm kneeling next to my mother and I'm thinking about the war. Every time I look at that confessional, I think about the war. They're both boxes, I think. Both the confessional and the coffin they buried my pal Bob in—they're both boxes. And they're both wooden, possibly both pine. The only difference, I tell myself, is that the confessional is standing on its side.

For some reason, you narrated this passage through Lou's voice. If this surprised you, relax:

You are just trying out voices, and this exercise took only a few minutes. After your second trial paragraph, you thought Lou wanted to speak more, so unconsciously you must have decided to let him try narrating. "Fair enough," you should tell yourself. To deal with what happened, make notes on the sample. As you read it, were you pleased with the way having Lou tell the story sounded? Did you feel, as you wrote it, that Lou could go on speaking for pages, with little effort on your part? Or did his words come slowly and haltingly? Take another break, and see what happens on your fifth try.

Lou talks too much. That's his problem. That's why he lies in the first place. If he didn't talk and lie so much I never would have asked him to go to confession. After all, we're all getting old. I might get a clean bill of health every time I see Doctor Ted, but Lou's a smoker and a drinker and, well, you just never know.

Again, read out loud and make notes. If you want to try Sally's voice—or Lou's—in more paragraphs, by all means do so. Then read each again, to help you make further necessary decisions. Maybe you wrote your fifth sample quickly, but you'd like to combine its more serious tone with the events of the first sample. If so, try another paragraph to see whether you can pull that off. Maybe you like the fourth sample more every time you read it, and you'd like to write a quick character dossier for Bob, who, prior to this exercise, hadn't existed. If so, do that. Make the adjustments you feel are necessary. Your goal at this stage is to feel comfortable writing in Sally's voice, and to be eager to write your rough draft.

Since developing style—or a particular voice for a character's first-person narrative—is a hit-or-miss process, here are some tips that might help:

1) Don't let the fact that you might not have a character's voice down *perfectly* keep you from writing the rough draft of his or her first-person narrative; think of rough-draft writing as a worthwhile discovery process.

2) If you hear a character's voice distinctly but you simply cannot put it into words on paper, think of yourself as a secretary and the voice as your boss—and take dictation. If the voice interrupts this dictation to give you directions on how it wants you to do your job, jot those directions in your journal or at the bottom of that particular page of your text.

3) Your writing style may not sound like *your* speaking voice. If so, good for you. Reflecting your speaking voice in a fiction piece might be inappropriate and become tiresome—to you and your reader; also, most of the time it won't accurately reflect the thoughts and dialogue of your characters.

4) If replicating any voice creates good fiction quickly, distinctly, and consistently, it is serving you well—so let it speak by writing it down. You can always fine-tune it later.

5) Occasional underlining or capitalization in

your manuscript may, as it emphasizes words or phrases, help you develop style or refine a character's first-person narrative voice. Use contractions, run-ons, fragments, and deliberate misspellings, if appropriate to the character speaking. You'll probably want to edit out these "crutches" later in the process of writing the story.

6) If you've selected a first-person narrative voice for a piece and find yourself writing about events other than those on your most recent event chain, pursue these new events briefly, then try to steer back onto the course of your plot. If, as you write, you continue to veer from your plot, do so for only as long as you can write quickly, then consider changing or abandoning your event chain. Or: try to strike a compromise between the narrative you'd planned and the new one you've just created. Or: consider using one of your two plot options for your next short story or novel.

7) Above all, remember that a distinctive voice can often mean the difference between a story or novel that an editor admires, and one that an editor accepts and publishes. If as you read it aloud, the "voice" you have created sounds strong, urgent, but a bit strange, don't be upset or judgmental. Let it help you write. Voice needn't be formal or "educated." If you let it say what it wants to say, it can add rhythm, entertainment, and pace to your fiction—as well as enjoyment to your readers.

"Characters should interact with setting as much as they do with one another."

‖ 5

Establishing a Lively Setting

SOME BEGINNING WRITERS believe that setting should be established at the outset of a work of fiction, and that it loses importance as a piece develops. They're wrong. Or at least they're cheating themselves, their fiction, and their readers. Setting is as crucial an element as character and plot. In the best fiction, setting interacts with character and plot to produce tension, suspense, and reader satisfaction.

The word "setting" is somewhat of a misnomer, because it implies something *set*—something upon which characters act. Perhaps a better term for it is "environment," which implies a *living* place that can react as well as act. The best settings (or environments) can comfort, provide for, and/or kill a character; they can complicate plots and lead to dramatic and poignant endings.

Setting has primary importance in stories that satisfy readers, so writers should choose their settings carefully.

Study your dossiers, event chain, and voice samples to determine your setting. If your main character is overworked or prone to anxiety, you might want to reflect this by setting your piece in a busy city. Or maybe your particular character's thoughts would sound louder to you if "heard" against the backdrop of a silent desert. Since this is up to you, take advantage of the fact and make your decision logically. Don't set your story in a studio apartment because you're sitting in one as you write.

Plot can dictate setting in the sense that certain events can happen only in certain places: Obviously that car accident you want to write about couldn't happen in a forest. On the other hand, consider going against the grain of probability by using setting to spice up plot: Tell yourself that something *like* a car accident could happen in something like a forest—in fact, theoretically, two *motorcycles* could collide in the woods. More likely, a person riding a motorcycle through the woods could hit an unseen rock—or even a bear carcass—and flip over. Or, if you don't know much about motorcycles but want to be sure the action you describe is authentic, you might decide to use bicycles instead of motorcycles.

Whatever setting you choose, adjust your event lists to fit it. Let setting interact with plot *before* you begin drafting, so as your story or novel develops, plot and setting interact organically.

But don't stop there. Consider character, too. Why would someone ride a bike through the woods? Search your character dossiers for a hint of the kind of *motivation* that relates to your setting. Maybe one of your minor characters climbed down a fire escape in grade school on a dare. Perhaps this personality trait, which you'd ignored until now, could be attributed to your main character: Possibly someone has dared your main character to ride a bike from one end of a densely wooded area to the other. Or maybe someone bet your main character that she couldn't make it in less than five minutes, so she's trying to do it to win the bet. Or your main character is using a bike to reach another character quickly, because the other character is suffering a stroke. Wait a second: How about making your main character an emergency medical technician (E.M.T.) who's being rushed through a short-cut in the woods by a Hell's Angel on a motorcycle to get to the stroke victim.

Once a combination of plot, setting, and characters appeals to you, consider narrative voice. Would the Hell's Angel's voice be the most compelling— especially if the stroke victim were his wife? And now that you've been considering setting and it's shifted to the woods, what's been happening to your nice, simple plot about a car accident? It didn't hold up.

But much of it might be salvageable: Your main character—the E.M.T.—can still be the divorced woman for whom you made a 200-entry character dossier. Also, you could use a good part of your most recent event chain. While your main character might still save a life, now it would take place in the more restricted surroundings of the woods. And you could still end with having your main character telephoning her ex-husband, but now she might be calling from a Hell's Angel's apartment, and the Hell's Angel might get to say that poignant last line.

Notice how setting, character, and plot intermingle here to affect all aspects of the story: When you chose the woods for your setting, the car accident had to be changed to events involving a motorcycle and a motorcycle rider, and this would make it necessary for some of your dialogue to be more earthy and straightforward. Thus simply by changing the setting, the characters, plot, and dialogue also had to change.

Once you've chosen the setting for your fiction—and allowed it to affect and even improve your fiction—search this setting for sensory details. List as many of these as you can in *specific* terms. Here's the beginning of a list of sensory details that flesh out a possible setting:

1. orange stain on ceiling (sight)
2. shrill whistle of copper teapot (sound)

3. purple shag carpet covered with white cat hair (sight)

4. humid breeze blowing through bullet hole in window (sound and touch)

5. hiss of skidding jeep tires outside (sound)

6. odor of unchanged cat litter box (smell)

7. glass of budded daffodils on table—no water in vase (sight, smell)

8. smooth hi-gloss pink walls (touch, sight)

9. a tin can full of Canadian pennies on antique dresser (sight)

10. crumpled green doily on floor near neatly made twin bed (sight)

Read your list for *enhancing details*. These are items that, when imagined, make the scene surrounding them more vivid. For example, if you write "AstroTurf doormat on the farmhouse's front porch," the average reader gets a sense of not only the doormat, but also the porch (concrete and a little muddy), the outside of the farmhouse (at least fifty years old), the inside (knickknacks on the walls), and maybe even the farm itself (rows and rows of bright green shoulder-high cornstalks).

Because readers tend to generalize from details they see—a common tendency—try to select specific details for your setting that will make the readers' experience more satisfying. How do you know which details will enhance a reader's first impression? You never do know for sure. But by reading your lists of setting details, by closing your eyes and "seeing" how quickly and extensively your imagination expands, you may develop an instinct for choosing the details that will bring the reactions and responses from your readers that you are aiming for. If you write "shiny black diskette," the readers will move from the image, probably quite slowly, to a generic computer and perhaps to a desk. If you write "spoon smeared with cookie batter," a reader is likely to picture a wooden spoon, thick batter, a yellow plastic bag of chocolate chips, a glass mixing bowl full of cloudy water in a cluttered sink, a Formica countertop dusted with flour, a large kitchen table, and a half-open window through which children's laughter is heard and the smell of fertilizer wafts in.

It could be that reader *emotion* causes some details to generate new images more than others. Or it could be that readers and writers share a collective memory. What's important to you as you choose details for your fiction is that you strive to paint entire pictures with single, emotional brush strokes.

Here are some practical tips that might address your particular problems with setting:

1) To practice using all five of the senses in conveying details to your readers, take a piece of trash from the rubbish container in your kitchen. If you find this too unpleasant, note the emotional power that simple *objects* can have merely by being in a certain place. Then write at least two pages in which you describe the piece of trash. If you think that two pages would be too long for what you have to say, you're wrong. Study it closely: Weigh it, smell it, bounce it, measure it, squeeze it, look at it upside

down; listen when you crush it, roll it, and smash it. If you can't bring yourself to taste it, ask yourself why not—then at least imagine how it *might* taste. Use similes and metaphors to help you when you feel like writing the word "indescribable." If you can't make trash interesting, your descriptive skills will never do justice to beauty.

2) Watch out for overreliance on *visual* detail in fiction. If you don't use other senses in your story, close your eyes to force yourself to create setting details that involve those other senses. Or, give your point-of-view character a deficiency in one of the five senses and allow this deficiency to intensify the other types of details in your narrative.

3) Consider reducing the scope of your setting. Imagining a background with confining boundaries often helps you concentrate on the details within it. Additionally, the boundaries may themselves offer details with which you can embellish your fiction. (The sag of the barbed wire fence might work better than the crackling cornstalks in the field.) Finally, the smaller the space available for your characters, the more tension their tale will produce. For example, a story of two enemies trapped in an elevator together is certain to be more suspenseful and interesting than if it were set in a field.

4) If you're having trouble imagining specific details, visit an actual place similar to the setting you're using in your fiction. Notice what you *didn't* expect to experience there, then figure out what sense will convey it most effectively. Perhaps your

setting is a garage, and when you visit an actual garage you're surprised to see a dusty pool table in the corner. Maybe the best way to describe this pool table is by smell rather than sight: If you concentrate on its smell, you might come to realize that it is coming from one of the pool table's pockets— which could lead your character through some interesting dialogue and action.

5) Stay away from clichéd settings. The thunderstorm at night is overused in murder mysteries; the hot summer night in the city is a familiar backdrop for the gang rumble. Let your legal battle erupt in a massage parlor rather than a paneled courtroom; show that first kiss in a crowded bingo parlor instead of a beach at sunset; allow the crucial championship soccer game to be played in an abandoned airplane hangar. Note how shifting events to unlikely places can enrich plot—because it forces you to create character motivations and plot complications that reveal why the event happened *there* rather than where it was expected.

6) Don't forget the value of color. Remember that each color has an infinite number of shades.

7) Characters' imaginations can help you spice up the description of an otherwise "plain" setting. Contrasting a character's thoughts about where she wants to be with where she is can create an evocative mix of details.

8) If you're using flashbacks, use setting details to help trigger the flashback itself. Should Len need to remember the fishing trip during which

his father died, put a fishing boat in your present scene to take your reader into Len's thoughts.

9) Use setting to help you create similes. If the background is a desert, Sasha's "green eyes" can become "eyes the gray-green of the barrelhead cactus at her feet," thus giving your reader a precise *and* economically worded detail about both setting and character.

10) Remember that even details *not* mentioned can suggest a facet of your character's psyche. If your story written from Jay's point of view is set at the edge of a cliff but the narrative doesn't mention details about the gorge below, your readers could *feel* Jay's fear of heights without ever having it mentioned in dialogue.

11) Prolonged description of setting—particularly at the beginning of a fiction piece—can sometimes slow down the momentum of your plot. If you find your description of the setting going on and on in your first draft, allow it to do so, but then, as you revise, break it up and sprinkle various details throughout. In deciding where to put a certain detail, take into account the possible symbolic or emotional effects that detail will have on your characters and readers.

12) Use setting details to slow down your characters and thereby to heighten suspense. If plot is a high-hurdle race, your setting should provide the hurdles.

13) If you are using more than one setting in a short story, remember that shifting from one setting to another can slow the pace of your narrative,

so consider merging two settings into one. Emma's tomato garden will prove more interesting if she's planted it near the old baseball diamond.

14) Occasionally, you can allow your characters to describe the details of your setting through dialogue. This helps readers feel an emotional connection with your characters' sense of place.

15) In general, setting should be woven into the entire fabric of your story in a way that affects your plot. Characters should interact with setting as much as they do with one another. As they change and the setting changes, their emotional reactions should vary. They should observe the key details of the setting through all of their senses, thereby enriching your fiction.

"Showing heightens the suspense and tension of a short story or novel; telling makes a work of fiction uninteresting and flat."

‖ 6

Action and Images

THE ADVICE TO FICTION WRITERS—"Show, don't tell"—has probably been given thousands of times. Beginning writers have nodded in agreement, often with only a vague notion of the meaning of this timeworn, but valid, rule.

"Show, don't tell" encapsulates the wisdom that a fiction writer can best satisfy a reader by conveying characters' emotions through specific actions, gestures, facial expressions, speech, or dialogue. Probably the best word to keep in mind when striving to show rather than tell is "specific," because this lends uniqueness, and enlivens and distinguishes what might otherwise be average, clichéd works of fiction.

Since nearly every *basic* story has been written hundreds of times, what makes a tiny percentage of stories memorable and brings satisfaction to readers is how an old story is *re*told. Imagine you are a fiction editor, facing several stacks of manuscripts, most of them dull confessions of love, divorce, and death. Halfway through your first stack, you'll begin to get the impression that the average writer has simply rehashed hackneyed plots, or has, in a sense, used you as a psychotherapist. What you are looking for, craving as a reader, is entertainment.

Fiction editors are responsible for the entertainment—or at least the stimulation—of readers who read fiction as an escape from—or at least to make sense of—their own monotonous, possibly unbearable, daily lives. The last thing readers need or want is to be bored by someone else's experiences. Responsible editors therefore reject manuscripts that "tell" and don't "show."

When you tell about an emotion in fiction, you ruin the momentary mystery about a character: If the character were the star of a movie, the *amateurish* movie reviewer, while recommending the movie, might give away the main character's ultimate fate. One of the reasons people read novels (or go to movies) is for the pleasure of speculating about what might happen. Reader anticipation is what makes publishers take risks in publishing fiction they hope readers will buy. *Showing* heightens the suspense and tension of a short story or novel; *telling* makes a work of fiction uninteresting and flat.

What this means to you as a fiction writer is that if you want to succeed, you have to make sure that are you producing entertainment. You will accomplish this by including specific actions, dialogue, thoughts, and sensory details in your novels and short stories.

The "show, don't tell" rule, in the sense that it prescribes using *specific detail,* applies to all types of fiction writing, regardless of sentence length, narrative style, complexity of plot, or characterization. The enemy of this rule is not long sentences, but sentences that are vague and carelessly constructed or written in language full of clichés.

You might think, "I read published stories that *tell* all the time. Why should I take the trouble to show?" The answer: Publication does not equal reader satisfaction. Next time you read a published story you *love,* reread your favorite parts of it. Chances are that you'll select its specific physical and emotional details, that you'll be rereading a scene that shows.

What can you do to improve your ability to show? Several exercises will help. First, go to a place full of people (a supermarket, a subway stop, a crowded theater lobby, a ball game, a party), and observe their expressions, postures, and gestures. Try to guess their emotions and thoughts. This won't be difficult or feel unnatural because, whether you've realized it or not, you've been reading body language all your life.

Supplement your "people-reading" by creating words in your mind that express what you imagine your subjects are thinking. If they're conversing, imagine their dialogue. If you mumble what you're creating, good for you: You are describing body language in specific words. If you're ambitious, jot your gems in a small note pad. Make a game of reading people by taking turns doing it out loud with a friend. Or, observe your friends themselves, and, when they display an intriguing gesture or expression, ask them what they're thinking. Or, observe yourself. You're constantly using more gestures and expressions than you realize.

A second exercise involves listing human emotions or human conditions, as well as making a list of corresponding actions or images that show these emotions or conditions. For example:

Emotion/Condition	*Corresponding Action*
1. anger	throwing dish into TV screen
2. forgiveness	holding and squeezing another's hand
3. anxiety	wheezing
4. confusion	repeated blinking of eyes or looking around
5. exhaustion	slumping onto a couch
6. avoidance	changing subject of conversation

7.	tenderness	patting a person's back as he or she falls asleep
8.	attraction	focusing on a person's face, then looking away when the person returns the glance
9.	disappointment	shaking one's head and exhaling
10.	impatience	pacing
11.	nervousness	biting fingernails
12.	disbelief	rolling eyes
13.	deciding	squeezing temples with finger and thumb of one hand; furrowed brow
14.	preoccupation	checking watch during conversation
15.	proud success	flashing thumbs-up signal
16.	politeness	listening with raised eyebrows to the person speaking
17.	empathy	repeated nodding
18.	self-consciousness	sitting up straight and pressing back shoulders
19.	hesitancy	sliding fingers into back pockets
20.	irritation	wincing
21.	happiness	broad smile
22.	shyness	child chewing collar of T-shirt or tugging at hair

Notice that the above list does not include the more predictable examples of telling, such as "red-faced" for anger, "looking wide-eyed" for disbelief, and "tapping foot" for impatience, because expected gestures or expressions have minimal impact in fiction. On the other hand, extremely unusual gestures or expressions might baffle your reader, so aim for fresh ways to "show." These aren't always easy to come up with, but the effort is worth it.

Notice also that the above list contains no adverbs, because adverbs virtually always "tell." The adverb in the phrase "scratching the top of her head irritatedly" reveals the emotion, thereby ruining the satisfying guessing game for the reader.

When you use an adverb, you may be unconsciously aware that your gesture isn't expressing the emotion you want to convey. In other words, your instinct is fine, but your application is poor. To avoid this, replace the adverb with concrete specifics to describe the gesture.

Your list of emotions and corresponding physical gestures should never really be finished; you should always be watching for new ways to show rather than tell and looking for the freshest, most original examples. If you don't use them in your current fiction project, they'll be ready for a future one. Most important, by constantly looking for ways to show, you are training yourself to observe humanity rather than mechanically search for facts—which spells the difference between a fiction writer and a reporter.

Another way to show emotion in a work of fiction is to focus your attention (and your reader's) *away* from your characters' physical traits and on concrete images your setting provides. If your character picks up a coffee cup from which she finished drinking two pages earlier, your reader need not see her facial expression—or the nature of the gesture toward the cup—to know that she's nervous or preoccupied.

Remember also that when a narrative presents visual images and/or sounds, there's an implication that the character whose point of view the reader is following sees or hears what's audible or visible. Take advantage of this fact to sharpen your text. Don't write: "John stopped talking to watch the coffee cup fall." Write: "'I can't stand you,' John said, and tossed the coffee cup into the rock garden."

Here are some tips that may help you overcome the difficulties you may have with "show, don't tell":

1) If you can't think how to express an emotion, consider combining two gestures, or a gesture with a facial expression. Leaping to one's feet and clapping one's hands once means something other than merely applauding; wrinkling one's nose while pointing at someone shows distaste better than merely wrinkling one's nose; a kiss implies something different when the person kissed closes his or her eyes.

2) If you've found an original gesture or expression and you're not sure you're describing it as precisely as possible, try it in front of the mirror, keeping your notebook and pen handy. Vary the gesture or expression—and what you jot down—until you feel the emotion you are trying to convey in words is clear.

3) Test the phrasing of a particular way of "showing" by reading it to a friend and having him or her act out the gesture or expression. Then have him or her guess the emotion you're trying to express.

4) When people-reading, *push* the closeness of your observation beyond "normal" limits. If your friend Tim gives a thumbs-up to indicate good news, note that his thumb bends back at a ninety-five degree angle, the fingernail is chewed, the cuticle is red, and there's a quarter-inch scar on the first joint. But don't stop there: Make the cuticle *brick red,* the scar the shape of an upside-down U, his thumbprint swirled like the paisley on his black and orange satin tie. You probably won't use all of these observations in your ongoing fiction project, but you need to exercise your powers of observation *hard* to collect enough details to help you find the best one. And: "Runner-up" details might become usable in future fiction pieces.

5) Sometimes precise word choice in a line of dialogue can *show* more effectively than gestures.

6) Watch out for the buzz words that indicate telling. If you've written that any of your characters *feel, want, believe, hate, like,* or *love* something, you've taken the easy way out and will lessen your readers' reading pleasure. Don't solve this problem by deleting emotion. Instead, *represent* it.

7) Occasionally you can show with punctuation. Ellipses (. . .) indicate pauses or omissions (confusion, caution, or lying), and a dash (—) that cuts off dialogue conveys interruption (impatience, disre-

spect, anger). Use these marks sparingly to achieve the most impact.

8) Try to use a particular "showing" gesture only once in a fiction piece, but mentioning a "tick" repeatedly in describing a character can help sharpen the characterization or distinguish the person from others in a crowded scene. It can also add humor, but you run the risk of making your character into a caricature.

9) In general, if you have trouble coming up with actions or images or dialogue to convey emotions, study your character dossiers and picture your characters as *they* feel a particular emotion; then imagine what action or image *they* would show to reflect that emotion. Small but meaningful actions that link human beings to one another *show* what's important most effectively.

"Contrary to common belief, inspiration doesn't come to writers before *they begin to write, but* while *they are writing."*

‖ 7

Writing Your Rough Draft

YOU'VE CREATED lively characters, devised an engaging plot, determined your point-of-view character and narrative voice, developed a setting packed with sensory details, and practiced the art of showing rather than telling. Now it's time for you to sit in front of your keyboard and hope the sentences will flow. Maybe, though, that first sentence doesn't come. You believe you have "writer's block." If so, don't panic. You must move on! Consider a number of suggestions.

First, accept two premises: 1) There is no such thing as writer's block; 2) when you say you have writer's block, you are essentially saying, "I'm lazy."

This second premise might strike you as harsh—maybe you resent being called lazy. But any person who's learned to put words on paper can at least go through the motions of writing *something*; so claiming you have writer's block can only mean you'd prefer not to write. Refusal to believe in writer's block, on the other hand, eliminates your most professional-sounding—but often invalid—excuse. So, be tough on yourself. Think: I *can* really put my thoughts and ideas into words.

Specific exercises will stimulate your flow of words. One is free-writing, which is nonstop writing, during which you ignore all rules—of spelling, grammar, punctuation, logic, run-ons, usage—in order to fill one page (or ten) with words. Don't erase or cross out; just let your fingers keep moving until you've reached the number of pages you set out to write during that time period. If you feel stuck, write "I feel stuck" over and over, until you get bored enough to put down a new phrase or two. Here's an example:

> I am writing this because hey what is that noise I here if the place is bugged by the FBI what does that stand for really this is why colored purple feet little feats are best accomplished in big bites if the place what

about my story i feel stuck i feel stuck I can't write or can i if i let this go too fast to see then what this isn't making sense cents ha ha ha this too much for now keep going the bird is feeding on the grass i think

Free-writing works well in a journal, but you can also do it on a typewriter or word processor. You should do it in private so it's truly "free," and you're not worried about readers. The copy you produce may often be somewhat senseless—and should be—because it is basically a transcript of your mental process, which does *not* flow in perfectly ordered, logical, or punctuated sentences. But free-writing will release your tension, will introduce you to interesting first-person narrative voices, create occasional "diamonds" you can use when writing or revising a piece of fiction, and— perhaps most important—it will give you confidence that you can *always* get words down on paper.

Some writers free-write a page or two a day, every day, as a matter of course. They eventually find writing as natural as breathing. They scoff at the concept of writer's block, because their stacks of old journals prove they've written thousands of pages spontaneously. They view free-writing as athletes do daily workouts: It keeps them in shape and serves as a basis for the more demanding activities they'll face later. When it's time for them to write a rough draft, they free-write page after page, and then turn to a blank paper or screen and *produce.*

Free-writing even as little as a page serves as a mental and physical "warm up," so you can begin your rough draft: You will be able to write, temporarily ignoring grammar rules (you'll focus on these rules during the revision process), and your mind-hand coordination will be improved. When you read your free-writing, you might find that you've given yourself directions on how to start that first draft. Or maybe you already *have* started your rough draft: The string of words at the bottom of your paragraph or page of free-writing could prove to be just the right opening line for your manuscript.

To produce your rough draft, you can also use what is sometimes called "directed free-writing." This involves abandoning all rules of language—*except* that you continue to write words that are more or less telling your story.

Here's an example of directed free-writing:

> I'm supposed to write about patty and that Billy maybe I should change her name okay so how will the story start start it now Patty is waiting in the deli before her wedding for Billy he is late as he always is the words are all flowing or are they anyway she's waiting and angry because he is late again as he always is when he drinks and thats the problem with him in the first place then she thinks she hears a door creak and thinks its him but its the janitor what's his name again Ed so-and-so and he's walking toward her with flowers maybe carnations and she used to know him in grade school and he's crying

A third exercise you can try is "primed free-writing," based on the theory that a particular word or phrase can "prime the pump" and start the flow of words and thoughts that have been buried in your mind. Jotting down this word or phrase will get you started and motivate you to continue with whatever words come to your mind next. Whenever you feel your flow slow down, you write the word or phrase again and repeat the process.

"I could write" is a good phrase to use the first time you try primed free-writing, because it gives you a feeling of confidence and provides a certain rhythm. It has worked miracles for many writers, regardless of their attitude or skepticism toward the value of positive thinking or mantras. Here's an example of primed free-writing:

> I could write just about anything I could write a story or a novel or a screenplay I could write about Patty and Ed i could write that they were in the deli i could write them crying in the deli and laughing at some point i could write many things they could get married if they wanted i could make people laugh and cry i could write why Patty was in the deli in the first place that's a good question i should answer that i could write to answer that i could write for three hours today i could write tonight after the kids are asleep i could write about patty's fiance Bill oversleeping because he was drinking and that's why Patty's at the deli by herself when Ed walks in

Other primers you might consider using are "write," "I might," and "I will." Try each of these for a few pages, then try to come up with a few of your own. Chances are you'll discover a word or phrase that you'll find works for *you* for the rest of your writing life. And another major benefit is that you will no longer believe in writer's block—because primers are always there to start your flow, to keep it going, and to fight your negative attitude or fear of failure.

If you are doubtful about trying any of the above free-writing exercises, relax by promising yourself you won't show anyone what these exercises help you produce, and remind yourself that a page of *any* kind of free-writing usually takes the average *novice* only five to ten minutes; veteran free-writers have produced pages in less time than that. Try this valuable exercise, and you'll soon be able to write what's in your mind instead of freezing in front of your keyboard.

After you've warmed up by free-writing, get to work on the rough draft of your story or a chapter of your novel. Allow yourself a brief preparatory ritual (drinking a certain beverage from your favorite glass; closing or opening a door; saying a prayer; looking in the mirror and nodding; doing some push-ups—whatever works), but after that, begin to write! Even if you aren't "inspired," don't give up. Contrary to common belief, inspiration doesn't come to writers *before* they begin to write, but *while* they are writing: while they're sitting, eyes riveted on their last word, their fingers moving to stretch phrases into sentences. Even then, inspiration is a rare, fortuitous happening, and it might be nothing more than a feeling of satisfaction in what you've already written—in which case, you've earned it; it wasn't magically given to you. So, if you're waiting for inspiration, start writing in order to spark it. Anyone can say, "I have ideas for these great novels and short stories." Only when you've written can you provide documented proof.

Here are a few general practical tips to help you further as you draft a work of fiction:

1) If your rough draft isn't coming out exactly as you'd imagined or hoped, don't worry: This happens to most writers.

2) Feeling a little uncertain while writing your first draft is natural. Turn your uncertainty into enthusiastic curiosity about how your story will unfold; above all, keep writing and learning.

3) If you don't know how to get from point C in your narrative to point D, force it a bit. If this doesn't work, it may be that you've actually reached the end of that scene.

4) If you can't seem to get beyond the first paragraph, try writing a possible last sentence for the rough draft you're working on. Then figure out what will logically lead to that last line.

5) Search for the best words and phrases from your character dossiers, event chains, and sensory detail lists to find starters for hard-to-write sentences. This will give you a sense of achievement and motivate you to write more boldly as you progress.

6) Don't read your rough draft as you go along; wait until you've completed it. Use your desire to read it as a "carrot" to keep you going until the end.

7) If you get stuck at any time while drafting your fiction, write a letter to one of your characters and discuss your problem with him or her. Or have your main character write a postcard to a minor character—or vice versa. Or invent and write a phone conversation between two of your characters, and have them argue about who should get more attention in your next paragraph. Or make a list of items your character might buy if he or she had twenty dollars to spend in a convenience store.

8) If one of your minor characters begins to dominate the dialogue or starts a long, complicated monologue, consider changing your narrative voice to this character's—or use alternating points of view. Let this minor character say what's on his or her mind. If what he or she says seems entirely irrelevant, don't delete it or throw it away. It might become relevant during revision or serve as the basis for another fiction project.

9) Free-writing, directed free-writing, and primed free-writing are useful activities during "time-outs" from rough-draft writing.

10) If you don't feel comfortable while writing rough drafts, vary your environment slightly every day until you find one that works best for you. Try different rooms, times of the day or night, chair heights, and means of getting your story down (handwriting, typing, word processing). What happens when you eat as you write—or when you *don't* eat until you've written a certain number of words? Experiment cautiously, varying your intake of caffeine or nicotine. (Avoid alcohol, which might help

you produce a good page on a bad night but will, in the long run, slow down your productivity and your ability to write both rationally and artistically.)

Try different noise levels: Open or close windows and doors to regulate the sounds of traffic, rain, birds, dogs, and voices; listen to various kinds of music at different volumes. Your ideal set-up might call for a card table, a legal pad, six pencils without erasers to your left, the phone unplugged, the door closed, a cup of orange juice with two ice cubes set on the floor to your right, the shade drawn, the small window open only when it rains, your old transistor radio softly tuned in to a country western station. If something works, incorporate it. Two caveats, though: Don't procrastinate while you are trying to find the *perfect* environment in which to write. Also, don't assume that the ideal environment for your rough draft will also work as well for revision and proofreading.

The following tips highlight differences between drafting short stories and drafting novels:

1) When drafting a short story, do it in one sitting. When drafting a novel, write two pages a day, at the same time of day, five or six days a week. If you've written two pages of your novel and feel enthused enough to write more, do so, but when you quit for the day, you should know at least a half page of what will come next to get you started the following day.

2) When writing the rough draft of a novel, an "up and down" experience—easy days followed by tough ones—is common. Get through tough days

by knowing an easy day will probably follow. If you're writing a short story and you reach a "tough" period, just continue writing until you finish the story.

3) Write about your events in chronological order, if possible; if the scene you're working on for your short story seems fuzzy, get through it as best you can, and worry about details during the revision. If this happens when you're writing the rough draft of a novel, skip ahead or go back and write the chapters you feel eager to write and get them down on paper. This method works especially well if you've planned the novel to the end.

4) The beginnings of stories demand close attention to the introduction and description of setting and character. The beginnings of chapters in novels—except for the first few—will probably not be as front-loaded with descriptions of character and setting, because previous chapters have done this work.

5) When drafting a short story, don't be surprised if you lose enthusiasm after the first paragraph or page. When writing a novel, prepare to feel the "sag" after the first chapter or two—as well as a prolonged lack of excitement while writing pages 100 to 200. Drafting a short story is like jumping into chilly water: You dislike it at first, but get used to it the longer you stay in. Novel writing is like spelunking: Walking around the first bend of a cave—into darkness—demands commitment, and continuing through the middle, with no light visible from either end, demands trust. Fight these

difficult writing periods by assuring yourself that they are natural and by reminding yourself that your motivation will improve after you write through these tough times.

6) In writing a short story, don't change point of view in the middle of a scene; keep the viewpoint consistent, using *one* character's voice.

Shifts in point of view and narrative voice are common in novels, depending upon what the plot requires. This may seem to give the novelist an advantage, but using this "advantage" successfully requires skill. Novelists who use several narrative voices or points of view must make each of them distinct from one another. These writers must also make sure that the different narrative voices or points of view don't "blend" into one another over several hundred pages. This takes careful planning, immersion in the characters' personalities and their roles in the novel, and an "ear" for their differences.

7) Flashbacks in novels may take less space than those in short stories: In a single phrase, a flashback can refer to characters and events the reader has already encountered. Flashbacks in short stories, on the other hand, usually demand more space, because the characters and setting of the flashback need to be established within the flashback scene itself. To keep momentum in short stories, it is usually advisable to avoid flashbacks and set flashback scenes aside for future stories.

8) Short stories should end with an absolute "clincher": All crucial questions raised earlier in

the text should be answered by the end. On the other hand, the ends of novel chapters—except for the final one—should "clinch" what has gone before, but must also motivate continued reading by answering *some* questions, while raising one or two others. In the final chapter of a novel, of course, most of the remaining questions must be answered.

In terms of their openings and endings, chapters in novels are similar to *scenes* of a story. The significant difference between chapters and story scenes is that chapters relate only *part* of the whole, and, of course, are the length of an entire story.

9) In both novel writing and short story writing, remember the one cliché good writers are allowed to use: *Don't get it right; get it written.*

"If your thoughts about a possible change center on how difficult it will be to make, it's probably an advisable change."

‖ 8

Initial Revision

R EVISION IS THE MOST crucial step in writing publishable fiction. It may also be the most difficult. Unfortunately, beginning writers often receive praise from teachers or friends on various elements of their rough drafts of novels or novel chapters, but they are not told what needs to be fixed and how to fix it. As a result, many writers submit good *rough* drafts for publication, long before they are in publishable form—only to receive impersonal rejection slips. Sometimes aspiring writers stop writing because they don't believe they can achieve publication, when in fact they simply don't know how to revise, or they don't revise enough. These writers proofread for spelling or punctuation errors, maybe change a few words to make their manuscripts sound more "impressive," but then avoid the hard work involved in revision that may make the difference between the acceptance and rejection of their manuscripts.

Teaching and learning how to revise is difficult for several reasons. First, no two fiction pieces can or should be revised by any one formula. Second, all of the changes a rough draft will need may not be identifiable in one revision, because even the best initial revision often creates more need to revise. Third, writers may find doing revisions an emotionally unpleasant experience.

Revision by the process of trial and error often results in too many rejections, months of waiting for responses from editors, and, in some cases, years of emotional frustration. The often uncritical attachment inexperienced writers feel for their rough drafts is common and understandable; anyone who has done all that work is justifiably proud. But if you do feel this pride of accomplishment, don't you owe it the additional work it may need to get it accepted for publication?

To succeed as a fiction writer, channel your premature satisfaction with your rough draft into a drive to revise. Face the fact that you now have the extensive responsibility to spend time and effort in reworking your manuscript.

This chapter addresses only half of the responsibility of revision: major changes that entail whole segments of the rough draft. Make these changes *before* you begin to revise sentences or words. This will save you time: You don't want to reword a sentence that's part of a paragraph you'll delete later.

An approach to revision you might try first is to convince yourself—or at least pretend—that the first sentence of your draft is unacceptable. Inexperienced writers are often incapable of taking this step. "This first sentence of mine is too good to change," they tell themselves. If you say or think this, you're more than likely wrong—and you're certainly not ready to revise. So, put aside your draft, and start on another novel or story; or read published fiction until you're ready to address seriously the necessity of revising the rough draft.

Once you can at least *pretend* your first sentence is unacceptable, read ahead in your manuscript to find another, better sentence that might work as an opener, one that grabs the reader, conveys action and urgency, and hints at a character's goals. Consider using the various clauses of complex sentences or quotes in the middle of dialogue as your new starting point. Read your manuscript aloud; allow your gut feeling to help you recognize a good opening line when you hear it. When one registers, write "Start here?" in the margin and draw an arrow to that sentence's first word. Then read on for *another* possible opening line, and mark it the same way. Do this all the way through the short story or novel chapter, making at least three arrows. Don't ignore the possibility that your last sentence might be your best opener.

After you've read through your whole manuscript and found at least three alternate first lines, shift into reverse: Convince yourself that your last line must go. Read backward and find another sentence that conveys a sharp, "clinching" effect. Mark it with an arrow, and put the words "End here?" in the margin. Then read the entire piece backward to find at least three alternate last sentences.

Finding the right places for the arrows becomes easier as you proceed. Take satisfaction in the fact that you are accepting your responsibility to revise. Now choose your *best* opening line. While deciding, factor in the probability that your original opener sounds good only to *you*—possibly because of inertia or your reluctance to change. If deciding which is the best sentence is difficult for you, combine reason with your artistic instinct: Quickly jot down lists of strengths and weaknesses of each line in your margin or journal, then depend on your instincts to help you analyze what you've jotted down. If beginning with that line on page seven would require a lot of work, embrace the challenge as an opportunity.

Next, choose your best last line. Again, be both rational and artistic. If you find yourself adding a word or so to a particular line to make it the winner, fine. Do what's necessary to choose the best sentence.

Now comes the easy part: Cross out all the words above your new opening line and below your new last line. If you think your story absolutely *needs* any part of what you've crossed out and that you can fit it into the middle, mark up your draft to indicate where and how you might work it in.

Take courage! You are now working like a reviser. Your short story or novel is beginning to develop. But don't stop now. Reread your most recent event list and, with your new opening and closing lines in mind, consider deleting, adding, or reordering the events of your story. Concentrate on drama and suspense at this point: Delete events that merely take up space; add some that lead to magic moments; move your climax as far as possible toward the end of the list. Make notes on the list to reflect these changes, then make a revised list, adding *more* magic moments. Ask yourself if your story or chapter could have *two* climaxes—or a two-part climax to increase complexity, tension, and suspense. Or maybe even a *three*-part climax.

Use the revised event list as a guide to noting on your rough draft any significant changes you're considering. Contemplate crossing out scenes, sections, paragraphs, and sentences as possibilities rather than final decisions. Use arrows and notes to indicate how you might rearrange sections of your story. Ask yourself questions, jotting them down along with immediate responses in your margins. Should Jackson, your favorite minor character, be eliminated? Could he possibly become your main character? Could Lynn and Marie, your other minor characters, be merged into a single character to reduce confusion and increase character depth? Is your narrative losing its fizz on the second half of page ten? If so, why? Would a change in narrative voice bolster reader interest? How about using arrows to indicate alternate first and last lines of the various *sections* of your draft? Is the magic moment just before that basement door opens as magical as you can make it? Is all that dialogue on page four necessary? What if you used only half of it? Could you end the scene on page eleven with a different sensory detail? How about something more surprising? Should that final scene be set in an elevator rather than a car?

When you've marked up your manuscript to the point at which possibilities and questions are coming to mind quickly, do some directed free-writing to explore revision possibilities. Write until your thoughts stop flowing, then write half a page more. If possibilities don't come to mind quickly, try some primed free-writing linked by the words "I might" or "maybe." When questions and possibilities flow, don't stop thinking or writing—in your journal or on your manuscript—until your flow tapers off and you've written several answers to all of your questions. Then decide which revision possibilities will be most effective, and revise accordingly. Guide yourself with this rule of thumb: If your thoughts about a possible change center on how difficult it will be to make, it's probably an advisable change—so make it.

Here are a few practical tips that might help you get your revision on its way:

1) Don't revise sections of a rough draft on a word processor; work with a pencil on printed or typewritten copy. Part of the value of revision lies

in the notes you make in margins, the arrows you draw—and your recognition that you have to fix the story. Using a word processor discourages experimenting with deletions, because deletion on a word processor feels (and often is) more permanent than the act of lightly crossing out a paragraph or sentence with a pencil.

2) If you are satisfied with your rough draft for the most part, make several copies of it and put one in another room while you mark up another copy as explained above. Knowing that a "great" original version exists untouched will help you relax while you play with revision.

3) Set your alarm clock for four in the morning. When it rings, get out of bed, find a pencil, and read your draft. If you want to go back to sleep before you finish reading, figure out what this means.

4) If you are so pleased with your rough draft you can't bring yourself to mark it with a single arrow or change a word, crumple it up, uncrumple it, smooth it out, and pick up your pencil. Now: Why *not* draw an arrow to an alternate first sentence?

5) If your rough draft displeases you, crumple it up and throw it away. Then ask yourself if you'd rather write fiction or do something else. If that's the case, go ahead and do so, but realize that your chances of being a successful writer are dwindling by the second. When you feel ready to write again, retrieve your draft and get to work.

6) Don't revise with red markings; they might

remind you of a teacher you hated and stifle your thoughts. Use your favorite color, an odd color, or one that helps you relax. If you're afraid of making permanent markings, use a pencil with an eraser—but try not to use the eraser.

7) If your writing is sloppy as you rush to get your ideas for revision down, that's O.K.; you're better off having notes that are difficult to decipher than none at all.

8) Don't worry about the manuscript you've cluttered up with words, lines, and arrows. Be more concerned about a "too clean" rough draft.

9) Try to revise your rough draft in a place other than where you wrote it.

10) Put the rough drafts of two different fiction pieces on your desk. Find three new opening lines, then three new last lines for each. In other words, follow the process discussed above, but alternate from one story or chapter to another, as you move from stage to stage of the process. This will allow each to spark ideas for the other. If, during this process, your revision of one piece is flowing extremely well, let that flow continue until it tapers off. Then return to the first piece to "catch up."

11) When all else fails, try the old reliable: Put your rough draft in a drawer for a period of weeks or months. Write a new piece of fiction during this time, and if you come up with any ideas for revising the piece in the drawer, jot them in your journal—*but don't open that drawer.* When the weeks or months expire, grab a pencil, open the drawer, and mark up the manuscript immediately.

The following tips relate to the differences between initial revision of novels and that of short stories:

1) Novelists need more time than short story writers to stay away from their rough drafts before they begin to revise, because writing the draft of a novel requires much more time and persistence, and novelists need to recoup before they *want* to revise their work—or can face the daunting task of revising a long manuscript. When you've completed the rough draft of a novel, let at least six months pass before you begin to revise. If you don't do this, you'll line-edit and proofread entire chapters that don't belong in your book at all, a waste of time, a frustrating undertaking—and perhaps one that will kill your interest in it. Before you change a single comma, be ready—emotionally, intellectually, and physically—to delete segments of your manuscript and to rewrite every word.

Short story writers can usually draft Story A, plan and draft Story B, then return to Story A with sufficient change in perspective to revise.

2) Before you begin the revision of your novel, write a twenty-page synopsis of it without looking at the rough draft. If you create new material in this synopsis, look at it as revision possibilities. If you find that you've omitted parts of your draft in the synopsis, consider cutting or changing or deleting those sections in your revision, and possibly inserting some from the synopsis.

Before you revise a story, fill in the blanks in the following statement:

"_____" is the story of a _____

who _____.

If you can't fill in the blanks, you aren't ready to revise. When you fill in the blanks, make a list of ten to twenty significant changes for the story that will help it support your statement.

3) Look for areas in your manuscript that you've summarized rather than "scened out." For a short story, consider deleting these sections or turning them into moment-by-moment scenes. To encourage yourself to delete an irrelevant "pet" scene, jot it down in your journal as an idea for another story.

If you're writing a novel, expand brief summaries into longer, related subplots that have their own narrative momentum. Such long summaries can add texture to your manuscript and make it flow more like a novel.

4) Be cautious about reading other novels while you're revising yours. It can cause unintentional changes in your style that may make it amateurish or derivative.

However, there may be advantages to reading other fiction while revising your own, since it may spark ideas about refining your work. Let some time pass, and then use the new techniques you've learned, but make sure that they belong and don't appear forced.

5) For a novel, don't finish one or two chapters and show your manuscript to an agent or editor—

unless you've been offered a contract or representation conditional on the approval of sample chapters. Would-be novelists sometimes write only one chapter and show it to an expert, and then upon receiving negative criticism, quit writing the novel altogether. To prevent this, write at least 100 pages of your novel before you show it to anyone, so that, if you do receive feedback, you'll have the courage to apply those suggestions to your revision. Have faith that one day, when you've written and revised enough pages, you may become an expert yourself.

"The best writers make their manuscripts as nearly perfect as they can before *they submit them for publication."*

‖ 9

Revision: The Second Stage

A FTER YOU'VE MADE major changes in your rough draft—discovered new first and last lines, rearranged plot events, reshaped characters, significantly altered whole segments of your manuscript—you're ready to revise to refine. This second stage of revision might come a bit more naturally to you than the first. Having made major changes, you can now be a discriminating reviser (as opposed to a defender of your rough draft); you've invested so much work in your story or novel that you now want to make it the best it can be.

Your first concern at this stage of your revision is "word economy," which simply means "communication per word." Depending on the type of fiction you write, you might prefer defining it as "suspense per word" or "human interest per word," but the impact of any of these important elements can be increased by deleting, tightening, and cutting words, phrases, sentences, even paragraphs.

Optimal word economy will help you 1) counteract your readers' interruptions; 2) meet the constantly shrinking number of words magazine editors set for fiction; 3) avoid unwelcome rejections from editors who "never got to the good part."

First, cut all unnecessary or repeated words and phrases; trim introductory verbiage such as "However" and "On the other hand," unless needed for transition; use pronouns when they'll work as well as proper names. Read dialogue aloud to help you reword what does *not* sound natural in complete sentences; listen to conversations at parties, and notice how fragments of dialogue save space *and* add authenticity to your fiction; delete words from the beginnings and ends of your quoted lines. (Cut "Oh" and "Well" at the beginnings of dialogue.) Delete unnecessary dialogue tags and adverbs. Credit your reader with intelligence, and delete— or condense—exposition.

Change "but" and "and" to semicolons or periods. Combine consecutive sentences that describe mundane action (e.g., "John pushed his chair from the kitchen table. Then he stood up and walked to the telephone. Then he lifted the receiver.") into single sentences (e.g., "John rose, stepped to the phone, and answered it.") Where you've used two or more adjectives to modify one noun, choose the most unexpected and specific one and slash the others. Eliminate unneeded conjunctions, articles, prepositions, and other words that don't convey image or action. (Change "He was walking around when he found himself stepping on some money someone lost" to "He stepped on a ten-dollar bill.") Use verbs that convey precise action. Avoid where possible "again," a redundancy by definition; be sure your sentence really requires such words as "so," "even," "that," "then," "when," and "as." Restructure sentences to eliminate every weak word, and use strong verbs to convey your meaning.

Word economy can cut more than the fat: It might also nick bone and muscle. But don't worry. Your next stage—revising that will heighten specificity and clarity—will solve that problem.

Replace vague or confusing phrases with specific adjectives, nouns, and action verbs to make them crystal clear. For example, you might have just changed "Donna" to "she," but if there are two women in the previous sentence, you will need to use "Donna" to prevent confusion. Or perhaps you've economized so well that Bob is opening the hood of his Ford, but you never said he unfastened his seatbelt. Or: Adding "brass" before the word "doorknob" in a paragraph about Bob's new house will *increase* word economy—because it serves as an enhancing detail.

If adding some words after cutting others seems like a step backward, relax. Because you've just worn the hat of the word economizer, you've probably improved your work with more efficient and precise words. Sometimes cutting words results in oversimplification and a lack of clarity. Many experienced fiction writers read their manuscripts several times to check word economy, alternating each reading with a "go-through" for specificity and clarity. Further revision is *always* possible; the best writers make their manuscripts as nearly perfect as they can *before* they submit them for publication.

Once your text is economical, clear, and specific, study it for the dramatic impact of each sentence. In this go-through, you are treating each sentence as a story and trying to tell that story best. Make sure the first word grabs the reader. "Then the rope snapped. . ." does not open as urgently as "The thick rope snapped. . . ." See that the middle doesn't wander off the subject or sag. "The thick rope snapped while I thought about homework, and then the boat. . ." would work better without mentioning the homework. Make sure that the ending—the very last word—is concrete and/or thought-provoking, which will usually mean it's a noun or a verb. "The thick rope snapped, and the boat drifted three feet away from where it was" is not as dramatic as "The thick rope snapped and the boat drifted." (Note: Concern about dramatic impact explains why you shouldn't use passive verbs, and prepositions at the ends of sentences.)

To increase the drama of your sentences further, focus on the emotional effect of word order. Does each sentence convey human complexity in the most provocative manner? Revise accordingly.

Another approach that will sharpen your fiction entails varying the sentences in rhythm and length. You might have economical, specific, clear, dramatic sentences, but if they are not different in beat or rhythm, they may lull your reader to sleep! Make sure some sentences are short, some complex, some linked by semicolons, some using appositives. But don't be a slave to this rule: Consecutive sentences of the same structure can, at times, offer appealing and appropriate parallelism, and sometimes, depending on what's happening to your characters, you *deliberately* want your reader to follow the same rhythm for a paragraph or two. The similarity must be intentional. You don't want to write five consecutive sentences *accidentally* introduced by dependent introductory clauses—and then rationalize the result as poetic license.

The final step in refining your work is to proofread with a fresh and rested mind. Bolster your resolve to make your manuscript error free by reminding yourself that its next stop is an editor's desk. If you find proofreading difficult, be grateful: If proofing seems easy, you are probably overlooking typos and other items that should be corrected or changed.

Keep in mind that, first, you are not checking

for perfect sentences; you are studying every word and punctuation mark to make sure each is correct. If you are at all uncertain about the spelling of a word as you're proofreading, look it up in the dictionary.

Second, you are prone to miss a mistake in the words that follow a mistake you've just found, because finding an error and penciling in corrections breaks your concentration.

Third, you may create new mistakes when "fixing" typos, so always proofread the changes you've made as soon as you've made them.

Finally, since you are the author, you might be so familiar with the piece that you imagine words and punctuation are correct when they are not. So consider having someone else proofread for you. One caveat, however: A person who is not the author, or an experienced proofreader, however qualified, may not be as diligent as necessary.

As you review to clarify, don't ignore or brush aside other miscellaneous changes you intuitively feel are necessary. Let the improvements you've already made motivate you to make more. As your experience in revising fiction increases, you'll add your own rules and practices for revision. Making as many revisions as you can will bring your stories and novels that much closer to being publishable.

Here are some specific practical tips to help you as you revise to refine:

1) If you find fine-tuning sentences difficult, warm up on a draft of someone else's manuscript before you attack your own. Better still, practice on

published work. Sharpening a sentence in print will give you confidence—and remind you that revision can go on forever, even after a work is published!

2) Don't try to address all concerns—word economy, specificity and clarity, sentence drama, and sentence variety—in a single go-through. If you do, you're sure to miss something. Read once for each possible kind of change. Then read for each again—and again.

3) If you can't get yourself to revise for word economy, try reading with a pencil in hand and putting light parentheses around any part of the manuscript you *might* eliminate. Take a walk or eat a snack, then go back to your revisions, and read your sentences without the parenthetical sections. If the shorter version of a sentence is acceptable, cross out the words in the parentheses.

4) If you have a hard time inserting new words, phrases, or sentences to increase specificity and clarity, pencil in two or three optional phrases to replace your vague phrases. Put them in parentheses to remind yourself they're options—then, make those even more precise. Get a good night's sleep before you choose your "winners."

5) Leave a pencil and your most recent version beside your bed, and make tinkering with sentences, phrases, and words your "night reading." Or, try this between the time you wake up in the morning and the time you get out of bed.

6) When editing, use your own set of symbols: Underline what you think is perfect; put wavy lines

beneath parts that need redoing; circle typos. Improve the parts above the wavy lines by studying what you've underlined and imitating your success. Repeat what you've already done well. Don't worry about the circles until you've improved the words above the wavy lines.

7) Make two copies of your latest draft, and give one to a friend to read aloud to you. Listen for pauses, repetitions, paragraphs that move too quickly or slowly, monotone, glitches in intonation. See if the friend's brow wrinkles or he or she uses an index finger to assist reading. Make note of what needs to be changed on your copy, using wavy lines. Listen for misreadings as well—and, if they sound better than what's on your manuscript, consider them as possible changes.

8) Read your manuscript aloud, always with a pen or pencil in hand.

9) Motivate yourself with deadlines by which you must finish a specific go-through, but always be prepared to set a new deadline for a rereading you hadn't anticipated.

The following tips reflect differences between refining novels and short stories:

1) As you revise your short story, make sure the point of view and narrative voice are consistent: All words should sound as if they are spoken by the same person. If your story has two points of view, make sure each is distinct and necessary. Don't use more than two points of view.

As you revise your novel, consider adding texture to your narrative by using various points of view; the economical narration you've used successfully to write short stories can, after fifty to 100 pages of a novel, begin to tire your reader. Plan and organize these point-of-view shifts for artistic purposes: Determine which events would be most dramatic and/or engaging from a particular character's point of view.

If you shift point of view and narrator's voice, don't overdo it. Ten shifts in forty pages will confuse readers—and put your novel into the "experimental" category, generally considered unsalable.

2) Check for ambiguity. The number of acts in your plot will keep readers busy enough, so you must avoid uncertainties that will confuse them.

When writing a short story, allow yourself an occasional line or so of "controlled ambiguity," which might be called "double-meaning." It occurs when you want a sentence, usually in dialogue, to make *either* of two specific references, both of which would work well for your story, and both of which your average reader will find provocative. Using a word or phrase that has several meanings that you have not considered results in *uncontrolled ambiguity*. This leads to reader confusion and is one reason readers will stop reading your work.

3) If you want people to read your fiction from beginning to end, revise it more times than you think necessary—and then revise it again.

"Wanna-be writers don't work hard enough, and tend to give up too soon; real writers submit their manuscripts over and over until they achieve acceptance."

‖ 10

The Quest: Marketing

GETTING YOUR WORK published isn't a right. It will not just *happen*. *You* must do all you can to *make it happen*.

Only when you think your manuscript is flawless should you begin working on marketing. You'll need to submit it with *persistence* to get it accepted for publication. But *how* to sustain your efforts after receiving ten—or even twenty—rejections is the real problem.

The best way to maintain hope for your rejected fiction manuscript is to make sure you have invested extensive care and work into its production and revision. If you've done all the prewriting, writing, and revision you feel your manuscript needs to make it publishable, you'll be able to view a rejection slip merely as a temporary setback. Writers who have "cheated" their manuscripts of sufficient prewriting and revision are likely to have their work rejected, and they will stop submitting other pieces of fiction—perhaps because unconsciously, they realize that their "unfinished" manuscripts didn't deserve to be published. Editors don't decide which pieces of fiction are publishable; *writers* do. Wannabe writers don't work hard enough, and tend to give up too soon; real writers put heart and soul into their manuscripts, and submit over and over until they achieve acceptance, because they believe in what they've written.

Before you submit your fiction anywhere, ask yourself if you're willing to spend the time, money, and aggravation involved in submitting it to at least twenty editors for starters. (After all, publishing lore is full of anecdotes about best-selling novels and prize-winning stories that garnered over 100 rejection slips before the magic of acceptance happened.) Only when you have done enough revisions to make you willing to submit your manuscript at least twenty times is it worth taking a chance on submitting it.

When submitting your manuscript, don't ignore the basic mechanics: Single-space your name, address, phone number, and social security number in the upper left-hand corner of the first page of the manuscript; use one-inch margins; double-space your work on one side of each sheet of good-quality, plain white paper; never use onionskin. Use a cover page for novels, but not for short stories. Include a brief, professionally written cover letter in which you mention the title of your work and your previous fiction publications. If you're unpublished, don't mention it. Never chat about yourself in your cover letter. And *always* include a self-addressed, stamped envelope with sufficient postage for the editor's response—or you're unlikely to receive one or get your manuscript back.

Here are several less common, but nonetheless useful, tips and reminders about marketing:

1) Manuscripts sit on editors' desks in stacks. Work that is carelessly written, sloppy, unrevised or not proofread has little or no chance of consideration. Professionally presented work, free of typos and grammatical errors, competes for the limited publishing space in magazines and on book publishers' lists. The process by which "winners" are chosen may seem somewhat random and almost always unpredictable to the writer.

2) Publishing fiction is *not* a simple or rational process that obeys or follows one set of accepted rules, but this shouldn't bother you. After all, your novels and short stories deal with human emotions. Fiction—and its publication—is art.

3) Even if your fiction is accepted, don't expect to get rich. *Thousands* of writers submit to the

high-paying magazines and publishing houses. If you want to get published more quickly, submit to some of the smaller markets that usually pay poorly or not at all. Realistically, before you can expect to be well paid for a story or novel, you will have to have many of your short stories and novels published. And you'll have to devote a lot of time and spend a considerable amount of money submitting them before one hits the jackpot—and that may never happen!

4) Just before you've addressed your manila envelope to your prospective editor *by name*, with proper postage, and put your cover letter and SASE in the envelope, proofread your manuscript one last time. (Something about that "moment of no return" heightens your sensitivity to errors.)

5) *Never* pay anyone to publish your work. Earn publication with the quality of your fiction manuscript.

6) Some editors give preferential treatment to writers who've already published in minor markets. Don't resent this. Use it as motivation to get your work published in the smaller, "literary" publications. (If some writers higher up the ladder than you are doing better than you, don't curse the ladder; begin to climb it.)

7) Don't use cover letters to tell editors or agents what your manuscript means or why it's good. If you feel compelled to do this, revise your piece again until its quality and meaning speak for themselves.

8) Keep your cover letters brief. List publica-

tion credits when appropriate. Bear in mind that a letter with no publication credits listed might work better than one with two publications the editor might not respect. (Some editors prefer "discovering" someone previously "unpublished" to publishing someone who lists a teen romance story published in an unknown magazine.)

9) Don't try to "spice up" your cover letter with jokes, suicide threats, or sagas of poverty. Save these for your fiction.

10) As for submitting your manuscript to more than one publisher at a time, use common sense to make your own decisions on a case-by-case basis. Knowing that you can't sell first North American serial rights twice, consider the ethics of simultaneous submission. Remember that editors don't want to be embarrassed by rejection from writers, and that some of them hold pieces of fiction for long periods of time before making a decision. During these periods, other manuscripts are probably competing with yours.

Practical considerations can also help you decide whether to submit your work simultaneously: a) Given the prevalence of word processors and inexpensive copying machines, many authors submit their manuscripts to more than one publisher, possibly "beating you" to certain editors. b) Many magazines expressly allow simultaneous submissions. c) But if you get on an editor's bad side by doing this, you might as well forget about publication through him or her.

Sift through all of these considerations—ethical

and practical—before you decide your strategy in submitting your manuscript. By all means, pay editors at least one common courtesy: If you've submitted the same piece simultaneously to more than one editor, say so, and if someone accepts the work, *immediately* send the other editors notes that say, "Please withdraw 'Piece A' from consideration."

11) Don't telephone an editor unless he or she asks you to.

12) While waiting for responses regarding submitted fiction, channel your anxiety, hope, impatience, and wonderment into writing another story or planning your next novel. Nothing makes the days pass faster—or takes the edge off rejections—than having a new story or novel in the works.

13) Remember that you are submitting fiction to *human beings* rather than magazines and publishing houses. Remember, too, that the turnover of editors at magazines and publishing houses increases your opportunities for publication.

The following tips relate to the differences between marketing novels and marketing short stories:

1) Submit novels through agents (if you have one); most agents do not handle short stories unless they're by clients whose stories have appeared in large-circulation or prestigious magazines, or have had a novel published previously. Submit your short stories directly to magazines, but don't expect them to publish novellas unless their editorial guidelines and requirements indicate that they will consider them.

2) Read magazines before you submit your fiction to them.

3) Do everything possible to get the name and precise title of the *current* editor—correctly spelled—of the magazine to which you're submitting.

4) Quality of writing is only one factor agents and publishing houses consider in evaluating novels. Large houses are concerned with such marketing angles as timeliness, propriety of a manuscript's subject matter, and the age, gender, life experiences and distinction or celebrity of prospective authors. Also, agents and publishers consider whether authors show promise and have the ability to write consistently well in the future.

5) If you've written six novels and tried but failed to get any of them agented and/or published, don't mention that to prospective agents or editors when submitting your seventh novel. Call novel seven your first novel—and your six manuscripts "notes" for your second novel.

6) If an agent asks for an exclusive reading of your novel, comply by sending the manuscript and a letter in which you grant exclusivity *for a set period of time* (six to eight weeks). Don't try to reduce this period of exclusivity (you and your agent need to trust each other). If the period expires and you haven't received a response, drop a courteous note to the agent, asking if a response is forthcoming.

7) Once you have an agent, sell yourself *softly* to him or her. You are competing with your agent's other clients—and other new writers trying to get

agent representation. This means telling your agent about your minor successes (contests won, short stories published or anthologized, grants received) and not whining about the difficulties of the writing life. In other words, act like a professional, if you want to sustain a positive relationship with your agent.

8) If a magazine rejects one of your stories, don't immediately submit another story to *that* magazine, unless the editor asks you to do so. Send your rejected story to another magazine. This is advisable for several reasons: a) it's possible that understaffing, financial problems, and/or manuscript backlog caused the rejection of Story A by a given magazine and will also lead to the rejection of Story B; b) you don't want to be tagged as "too prolific to create quality fiction"; c) you don't want to bug editors.

9) If a magazine claims it responds to writers within a certain length of time, allow twice that amount of time to pass before you inquire about your manuscript. Send a brief, *polite* letter mentioning the title of your manuscript, the date of submission, the fact that you haven't received a response, and that you are enclosing a self-addressed, stamped postcard for the editor's convenience in responding to your inquiry. On the back of the postcard, write the following:

> Regarding Terry Writer's "Story A":
> _____ We have not received it.
> _____ We are still considering it.

_____ We have rejected it.
_____ We have accepted it.

Most editors won't mind checking one of these and dropping the card in the mail. Some, however, won't take time to do even that.

10) In general, as you send off your manuscripts, receive rejection slips, and question whether you will continue trying to get a certain fiction piece published, remember this:

Don't lose faith. Don't *ever* lose faith.